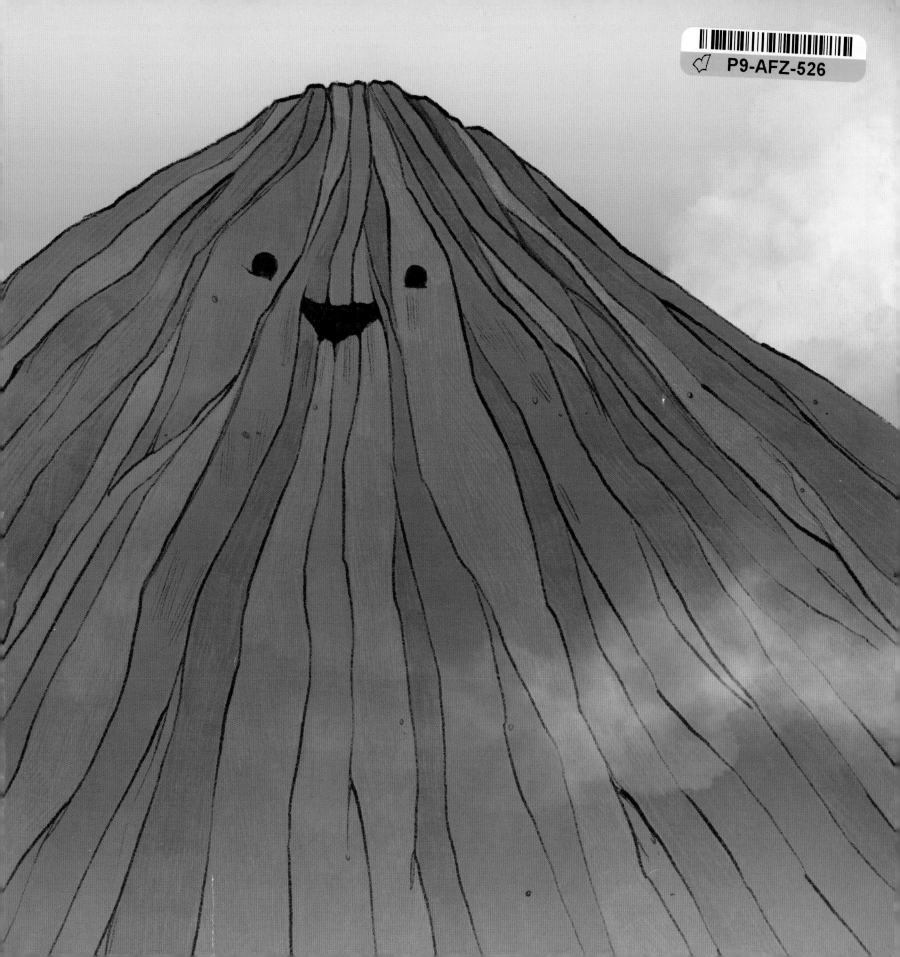

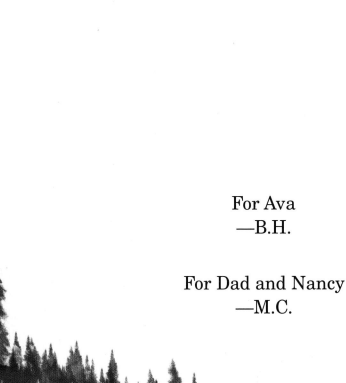

For Ava
—B.H.

For Dad and Nancy
—M.C.

Text copyright © 2022 by Bridget Heos
Jacket and interior illustrations copyright © 2022 by Mike Ciccotello

All rights reserved. Published in the United States by Crown Books for Young Readers, an imprint of Random House Children's Books,
a division of Penguin Random House LLC, New York.

Crown and the colophon are registered trademarks of Penguin Random House LLC.

Visit us on the Web! rhcbooks.com

Educators and librarians, for a variety of teaching tools, visit us at RHTeachersLibrarians.com

Library of Congress Cataloging-in-Publication Data is available upon request.
ISBN 978-0-593-30288-0 (trade) — ISBN 978-0-593-30289-7 (lib. bdg.) —
ISBN 978-0-593-30290-3 (ebook)

The text of this book is set in 16-point New Century Schoolbook.
The illustrations in this book were created digitally using the application Procreate on an iPad Pro with an Apple Pencil.

MANUFACTURED IN CHINA
10 9 8 7 6 5 4 3 2 1
First Edition

I'm a Volcano!

by Bridget Heos

illustrated by Mike Ciccotello

Crown Books for Young Readers

New York

Hi. I'm Volcano.

I may be quiet for now, but big things are happening beneath me.

Earth is made of layers of rock. It gets hotter the deeper you go.

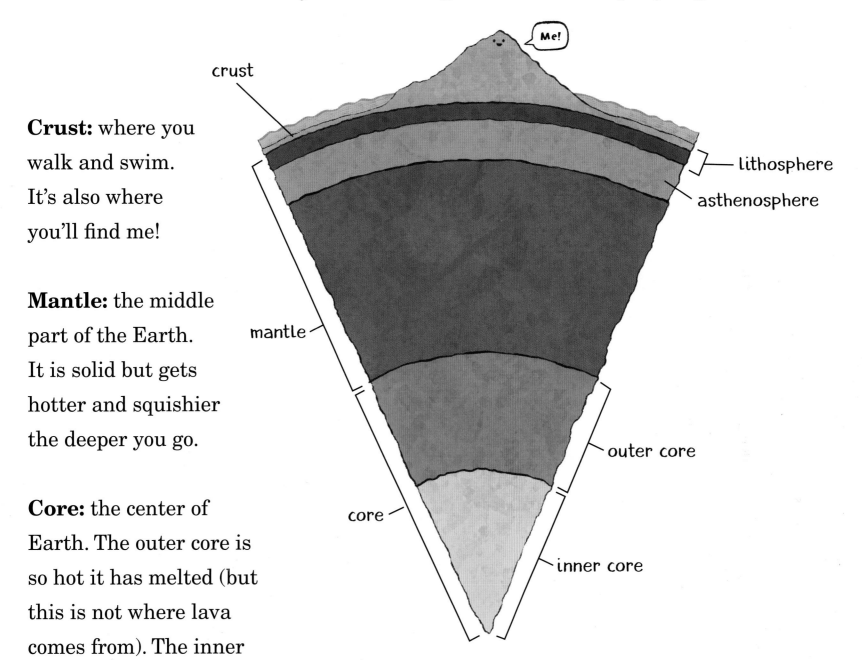

Me!

crust

lithosphere

asthenosphere

mantle

outer core

core

inner core

Crust: where you walk and swim. It's also where you'll find me!

Mantle: the middle part of the Earth. It is solid but gets hotter and squishier the deeper you go.

Core: the center of Earth. The outer core is so hot it has melted (but this is not where lava comes from). The inner core is even hotter but is solid because of all the pressure from the layers above it.

Lithosphere: a solid and hard layer formed where the crust sticks to the upper mantle.

Asthenosphere: a hot, squishy, playdough-like layer. THIS is where lava comes from.

EURASIAN PLATE

Here I am!

JUAN DE FUCA
PLATE

NORTH AMERICAN PLATE

PHILIPPINE
PLATE

COCOS
PLATE

You can't tell by looking at it, but
the lithosphere is broken! The pieces are
called plates. They look as if they fit together
like puzzle pieces, but they won't stay together
because they are in motion.

The pieces drift—sometimes closer to each
other, sometimes farther apart.

I am on a land plate. My plate is
drifting toward an ocean plate.

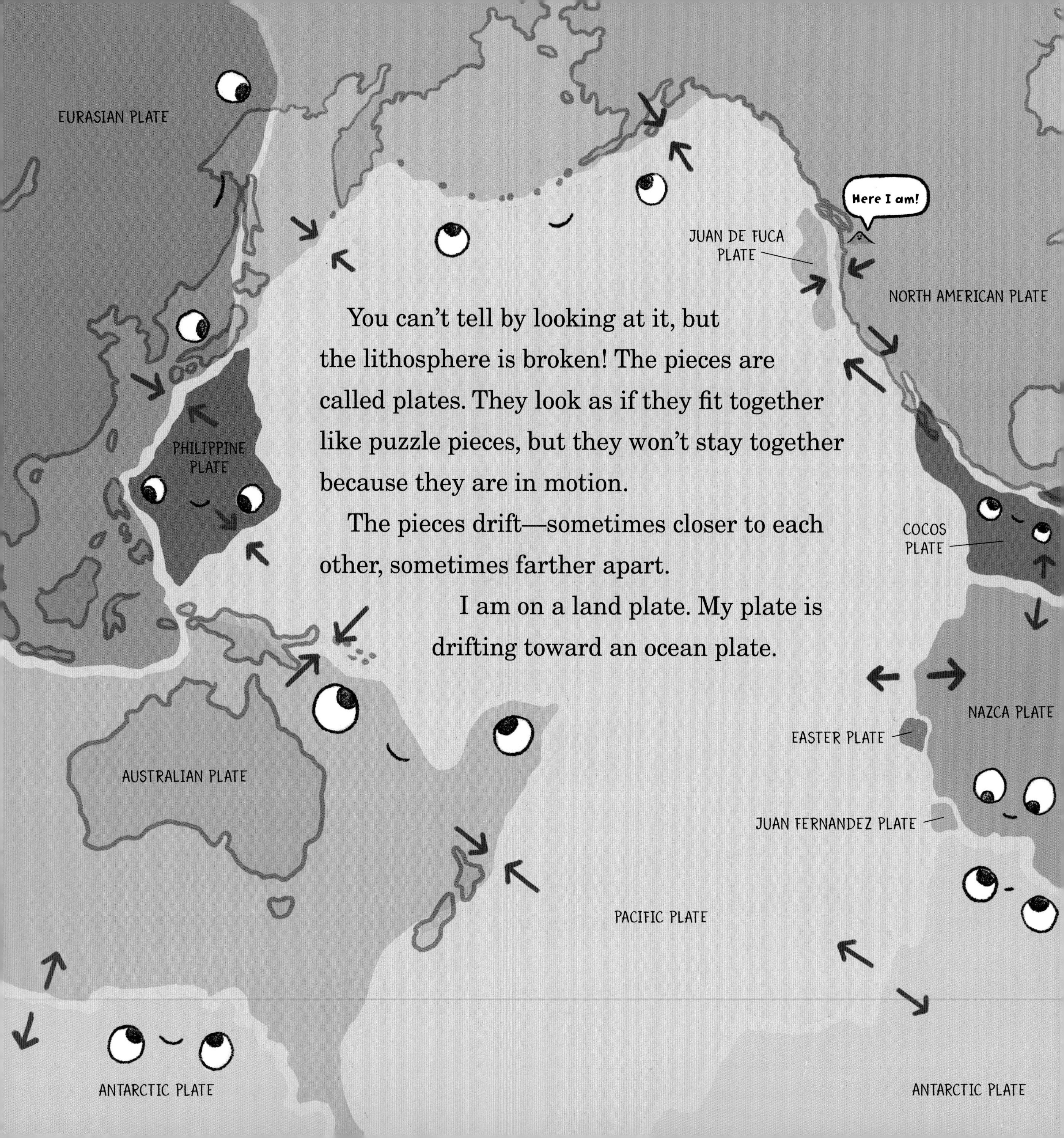

NAZCA PLATE

EASTER PLATE

AUSTRALIAN PLATE

JUAN FERNANDEZ PLATE

PACIFIC PLATE

ANTARCTIC PLATE

ANTARCTIC PLATE

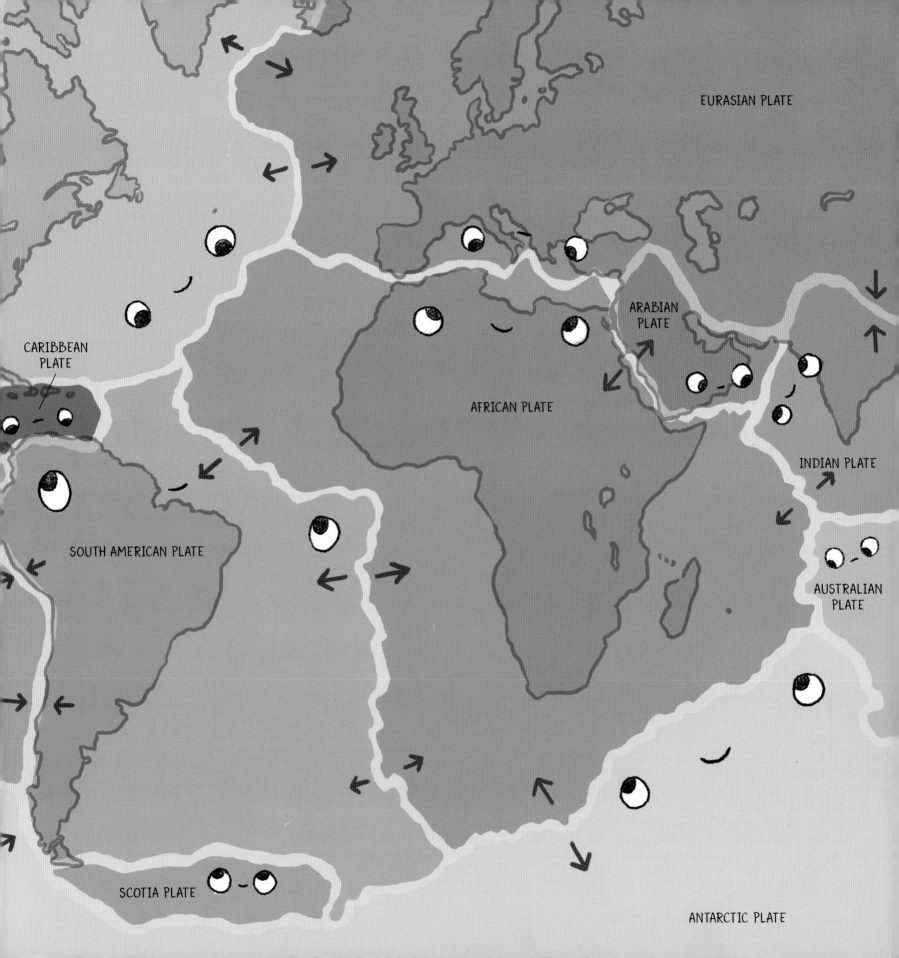

Bump! The ocean plate slips beneath

my plate into the squishy, hot asthenosphere.

The ocean plate is wet from all that—you guessed it—ocean water. When the asthenosphere heats up, the ocean plate "sweats" out its water. Water is a melter helper! It helps to melt the asthenosphere.

Voilà! Or should I say "voi-lava"?

Hot tip: magma is melted rock below ground. Once it reaches the surface, it is called lava.

ocean

lithosphere

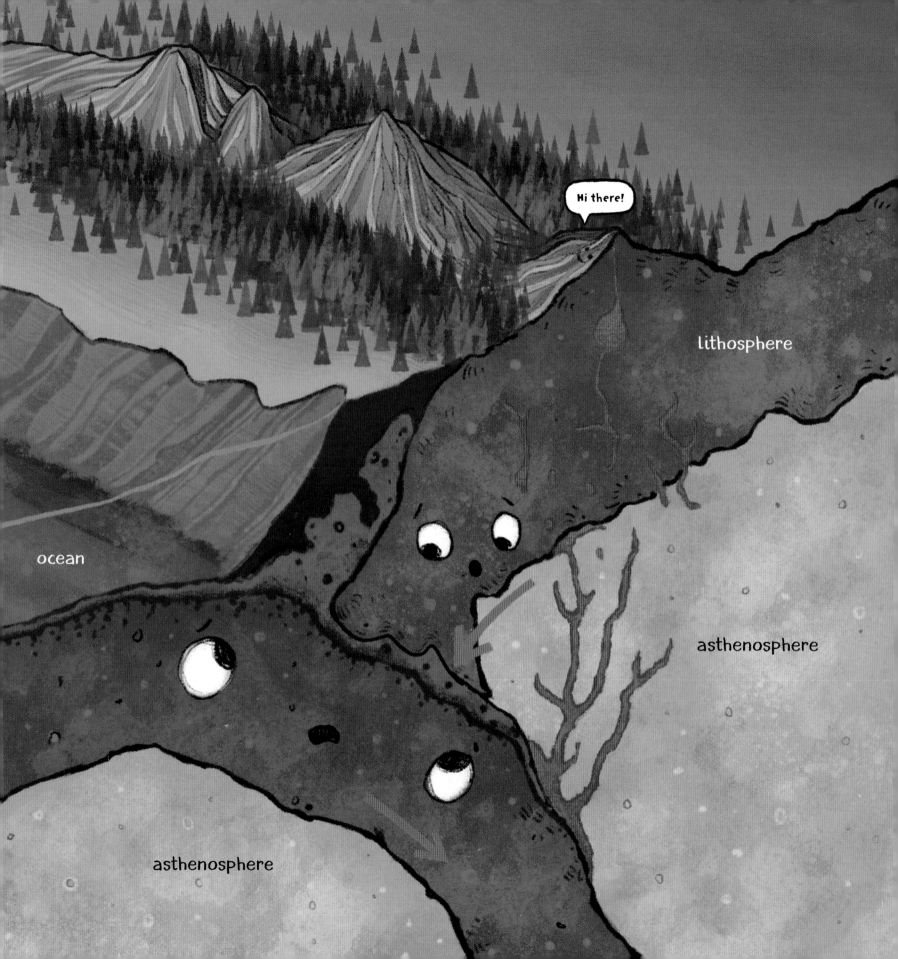

The magma rises. It collects in a magma chamber.

All magma contains gas bubbles. The thicker the magma, the harder it is for the bubbles to escape.

My magma is thiiiiiiick. The bubbles grow and grow and grow.

I'm like a shaken soda, ready to . . .

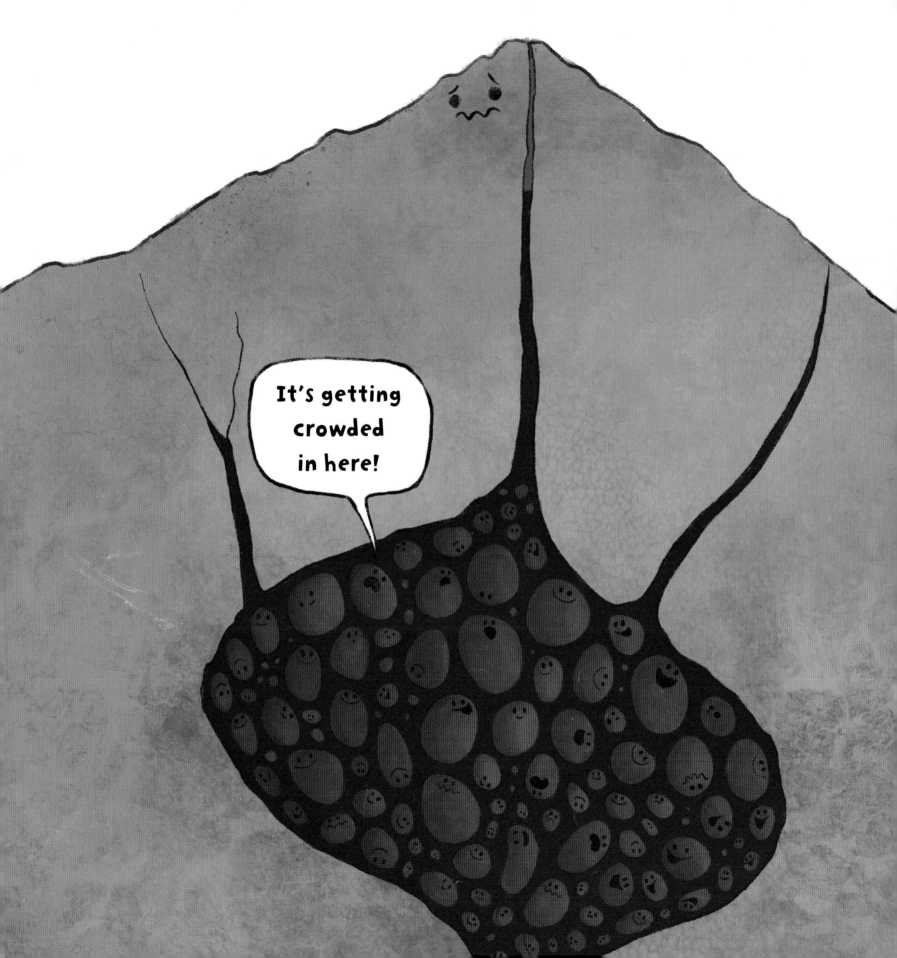

ODE!

The blast shatters the rock and magma inside me. They are now tiny pieces of glass and rock called volcanic ash. The blast shoots the volcanic ash many miles into the sky! What goes up must come . . .

This hot rush is called a pyroclastic flow. It is supercharged—speeding several hundred miles per hour.

Meanwhile, lava flows through my new crater. The debris and cooling lava settle around me. How do you like my new cone shape? Cool, right?

I AM cool. *And* I cool off—for a little while.

Until, rumble, rumble . . .

M!

Can you see why I'm known as a gray volcano?
Don't be scared! Scientists watch volcanoes
like me. They measure changes in my magma
with a special tool called a seismometer.

When I am ready to blow, scientists warn
people to go!

Why does the hot rock rise? Unlike Gray Volcano's colliding plates, my two plates are drifting apart, creating a new gap.

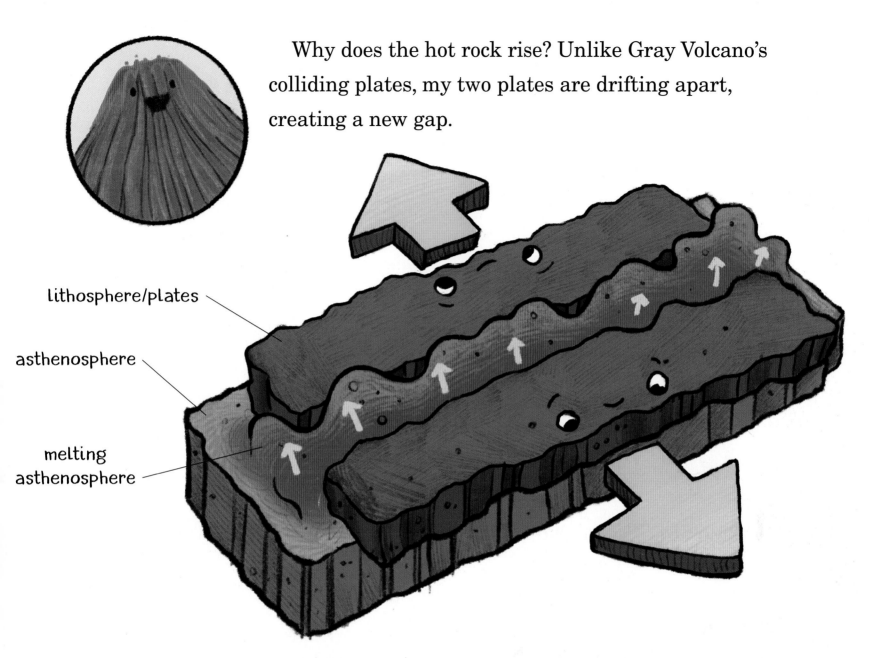

lithosphere/plates

asthenosphere

melting asthenosphere

Without so many rocks pressing down on it, the asthenosphere rises to fill the space and then melts. Lower pressure is a melter helper too.

But my ocean buddy doesn't know why things are heating up on the sea floor beneath him. When hot rock rises and then melts for unknown reasons, we call that a hot spot—ooh, so mysterious! Red volcanoes like me and my ocean pal have thinner and runnier magma than Gray Volcano. Because our magma doesn't have gas bubbles building up, we don't explode. Instead, we . . .

Being runnier, our lava travels faster and farther. But in most cases, it is still not THAT fast—you could even outrun it!

Fast or slow, our lava is literally red-hot—that's why we're called red volcanoes.

Scientists usually know when an eruption is coming and can warn people to get out of the way. Unfortunately, not all volcanoes are monitored equally, and they sometimes catch people by surprise. In that case, the volcano CAN be deadly.

With each eruption, the lava flows and cools, forming a mountain. If that mountain is in the ocean, over time, it may even become . . .

Although volcanoes like us can cause great destruction, we also
form beautiful habitats for plants, animals, and people like you!
I guess you could say that there is a lot to *lava* about volcanoes!

FAMOUS VOLCANOES

Mount Saint Helens

Mount Saint Helens in Washington State is a gray volcano. On May 18, 1980, an eruption blew volcanic ash and debris high in the sky. When the cloud collapsed, it melted the snow, creating a lahar—volcanic ash and debris mixed with water—that destroyed everything in its path. Fifty-seven people died in the eruption. Without prior warning, that number would have been much higher.

Status: This high-threat volcano is actively monitored.

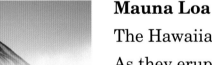

The Ring of Fire

The Ring of Fire is a horseshoe-shaped area that traces the western coasts of North and South America, the eastern coast of Asia, and off the eastern coast of Australia. Here, the Pacific and Nazca plates collide with or drift apart from different continental plates, causing earthquakes and volcanoes to form. There are around 450 volcanoes in the Ring of Fire, including Mount Saint Helens and Mount Fuji, and Okmok, Tambora, and Krakatoa.

Status: Many volcanoes in the Ring of Fire are active and monitored.

Mauna Loa

The Hawaiian Islands are a series of volcanoes that formed over a hot spot. As they erupted, they rose from the bottom of the sea to form islands. Mauna Loa is the world's largest active volcano and, measured from base to summit, one of two tallest (with Mauna Kea). It is so massive that the ocean floor sags under its weight. It is 5.5 miles (9 km) high from ocean floor to summit, and 10.5 miles (17 km) high if you include the sag.

Status: This active volcano is monitored for dangers such as lava flows, tsunamis, and more.

Yellowstone Supervolcano

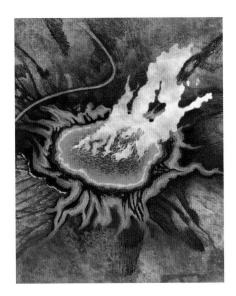

Yellowstone National Park in Wyoming, Montana, and Idaho sits atop a hot spot that formed a supervolcano—a volcano that produces more than 240 cubic miles (1,000 cubic km) of material in a single eruption! After such an eruption 600,000 years ago, the middle of the volcano collapsed, forming one of the largest calderas in the world. If this erupted again, it would most likely be a slow-moving lava flow—giving people time to clear out. (Note: Yellowstone is both a gray and red volcano.)

Status: Though the last eruption was 70,000 years ago, earthquakes, geysers, and more are evidence of an active volcano. It is monitored.

Mount Vesuvius

In AD 79, this gray volcano erupted unexpectedly, shooting ash and debris high in the sky. Next, a pyroclastic flow buried the ancient Roman cities of Pompeii and Herculaneum in layers of ash. Archaeologists later found hollow spaces in the ash—revealing body shapes of the dead.

Status: Mount Vesuvius last erupted in 1944 and is actively monitored.

Mount Nyiragongo

Mount Nyiragongo in the Democratic Republic of Congo is a rare lava lake volcano, one of only eight in the world. In 1977, the side of the crater cracked, draining the lake and sending lava down the volcano and into the city of Goma at up to 60 miles (100 km) per hour. It killed hundreds. In 2021, another eruption destroyed villages but stopped short of the city of Goma.

Status: Though considered one of the world's most dangerous volcanoes, scientific monitoring and communication about danger is hindered at times by political turmoil.

VOLCANOES THAT CHANGED HISTORY

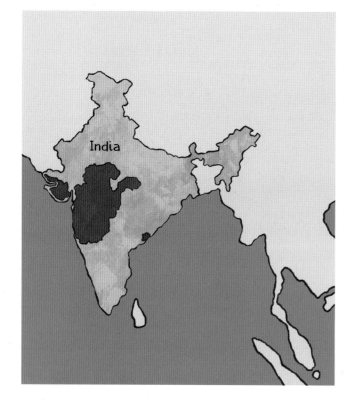

Deccan Traps
66 million years ago

Around the same time a giant asteroid likely caused dinosaurs to go extinct, a collection of volcanoes called the Deccan Traps erupted on an unthinkable scale. The eruptions lasted hundreds of thousands of years and blanketed the Indian subcontinent in 2 miles (3 km) of volcanic rock. Such eruptions would have sent gases into the atmosphere that initially cooled but later warmed the planet. Dinosaurs died out, mammals flourished, and humans evolved, so you might say this volcano didn't just change history, it created it.

Status: The hot spot is still active, but India has drifted far to the northeast of it. Piton de la Fournaise, a volcano on Réunion Island, now rests above the hot spot.

Okmok
43 BC

In 44 BC, Julius Caesar, ruler of the Roman Republic, was assassinated. The next year, a volcanic eruption in Alaska sent gases into the atmosphere that filtered out sunlight, resulting in two years of global cooling. The Roman Republic experienced extreme rain, snow, and cold. Food shortages and disease were rampant, causing the already unstable republic to collapse and give way to the Roman Empire.

Status: Recent eruptions show that Okmok is still an active volcano.

Tambora
1815

The Tambora eruption was the largest in recorded human history—producing 36 cubic miles (150 cubic km) of ash and debris. It killed 117,000 people on the host island and surrounding islands and buried the entire kingdom of Tambora. It also led to the year without a summer in 1816—causing crop failure and starvation around the world.

Status: Though subsequent eruptions have been smaller, Tambora is still an active volcano.

Krakatoa
1883

Heard 2,800 miles (4,500 km) away in Australia, the eruption of Krakatoa is thought to be the loudest noise in recorded history. The explosion destroyed the whole island! Though it is thought to have been uninhabited, the fallout reached people nearby and, even deadlier, its collapse spawned a tsunami that killed thousands. As with many of the volcanoes described here, Krakatoa also changed global weather.

Status: Though the island was destroyed, the volcano remains active and has formed a new island: Anak Krakatoa (Child of Krakatoa).

AN ILLUSTRATED VOLCANO

Crater—A crater forms where the ash and gas blasted out. If the blast caused the center of the volcano to collapse, this area is called a caldera.

Main vent—The path from the magma chamber to the opening is called the main vent.

Cone shape—Layers of hardened lava and ash from previous eruptions form a cone shape.

Side vent—Lava may also flow through a side vent.

Water—The hot asthenosphere causes the oceanic plate to sweat out the water it contains.

Magma chamber—Melted rock rises up and collects in the magma chamber.

Lithosphere—The crust and part of the upper mantle form the lithosphere. The lithosphere is broken into land and ocean plates that move toward or away from each other.

Asthenosphere—The asthenosphere is in a deeper part of the mantle. It is where magma forms. When two plates collide, the denser oceanic plate slips under the continental plate into the asthenosphere.

Crust, Mantle, Outer core, and Inner core—Earth has layers of rock that get hotter the deeper they are.

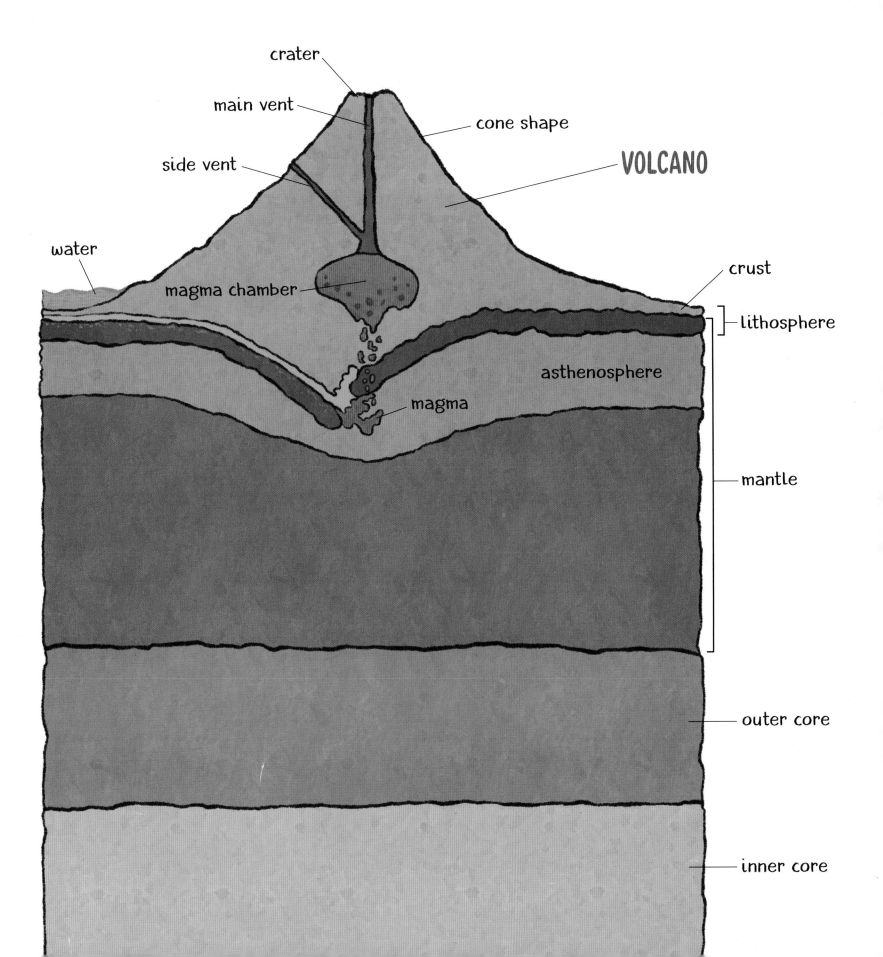

GLOSSARY

Asthenosphere—part of the mantle that is beneath the lithosphere. It is solid but soft, like playdough.

Crust—the top layer of rock on Earth

Gray volcano—a volcano that has explosive eruptions of gray ash

Hot spot—a place in the mantle where hot rock rises and melts

Inner core—the solid layer of rock at the center of the Earth

Lava—the name for magma when it is above ground—whether in liquid form or cooled solid state

Lithosphere—the crust and part of the upper mantle. It is broken up into plates that move atop the softer asthenosphere.

Magma—the name for melted rock when it is below ground

Mantle—the layer of rock between the crust and outer core

Outer core—the liquid layer of rock between the mantle and inner core

Plate—one of several pieces of the lithosphere that move toward and away from each other

Pressure—force applied to an object. For instance, rocks press down on the rocks below them, and the heavier the rocks, the more pressure they apply.

Pyroclastic flow—volcanic ash, gas, and debris that rushes down the side of a volcano after an explosive eruption

Red volcano—a volcano that typically erupts slowly, resulting in lava flows that appear red due to their heat

Rock—a solid mass made of minerals that occurs naturally in large quantities

Volcanic ash—a mixture of lava, rock, and glass fragments that forms during an explosive eruption

Volcano—an area on land or on the ocean floor that collects magma and erupts or has erupted in the past

FOR FURTHER READING

Cuthbert, Megan, and Jared Siemens. *How Volcanoes Shape the Earth.* Shaping Our Earth. New York: AV2, 2021.

Galat, Joan. *Erupt! 100 Fun Facts About Volcanoes.* New York: National Geographic, 2017.

Gibbons, Gail. *Volcanoes.* New York: Holiday House, 2022.

Rusch, Elizabeth, and K. E. Lewis. *Will It Blow?: Become a Volcano Detective at Mount St. Helens.* Seattle: Little Bigfoot, 2017.

Rustad, Martha Elizabeth Hillman. *Volcanoes.* Smithsonian Little Explorer. Washington, D.C.: Capstone, 2014.

SELECT BIBLIOGRAPHY

Camp, Vic. "Subduction Zone Volcanism." *How Volcanoes Work.* San Diego State University. sci.sdsu.edu /how_volcanoes_work/subducvolc_page.html.

"Effusive & Explosive Eruptions." *The Rock Cycle.* The Geological Society. www.geolsoc.org.uk/ks3/gsl /education/resources/rockcycle/page3599.html.

Encyclopedia of Volcanoes, The. Edited by Haraldur Sigurdsson, with the assistance of Bruce Houghton, Stephen R. McNutt, Hazel Rymer, and John Stix. London: Elsevier, 2015.

"How high can explosive eruptions go and how far can the debris and ash be spread?" Volcano World. Oregon State University. volcano.oregonstate.edu/faq/how-high-can-explosive-eruptions-go-and-how-far -can-debris-and-ash-be-spread.

Kenedi, Christopher A., Steven R. Brantley, James W. Hendley II, and Peter H. Stauffer. "Volcanic Ash Fall—A 'Hard Rain' of Abrasive Particles." U.S. Geological Survey. pubs.usgs.gov/fs/fs027-00/.

Lockwood, John P., and Richard W. Hazlett. *Volcanoes: Global Perspectives.* Oxford: Wiley-Blackwell, 2010.

O'Meara, Donna. *Volcano: A Visual Guide.* Buffalo, NY: Firefly, 2008.

Oskin, Becky. "Antarctic Lava Lake Huffs and Puffs Like a Sleeping Dragon." *Live Science.* April 22, 2014. livescience.com/45038-erebus-lava-lake-cycles-revealed.html.

"Volcano." National Park Service. December 29, 2019. nps.gov/yell/learn/nature/volcano.htm.

"Volcanoes." The Geological Society. 2017. www.geolsoc.org.uk/~/media/shared/documents/education%20 and%20careers/Resources/FactSheets/Volcanoes%20final.pdf?la=en.